CRIME SCIENCE

TERROR ALERT

Using Science to Fight Terrorism

CHERITON
CHILDREN'S BOOKS

Published in 2023 by **Cheriton Children's Books**
1 Bank Drive West, Shrewsbury, Shropshire, SY3 9DJ, UK

© 2023 Cheriton Children's Books

First Edition

Author: Sarah Eason
Designer: Paul Myerscough
Editor: Louisa Simmons
Proofreader: Ella Hammond

Printed in China

Please visit our website,
www.cheritonchildrensbooks.com
to see more of our high-quality books.

CONTENTS

CHAPTER 1

TERROR ALERT

Terrorism is any shocking act that causes mass destruction and loss of life. It can be carried out by organized terrorist groups or disgruntled individuals. Acts of terror take place throughout the world, and range from suicide and car bombings through mass shootings. Terrorism has no borders —for example it is just as much a problem in the United States as it is in the Middle East. Today, governments are more aware than ever of the need to be vigilant against terror attacks.

An Ongoing War

In the United States, the police, government, and **intelligence** agencies such as the Federal Bureau of Investigation (FBI) and the Central Intelligence Agency (CIA) all have a role to play in stopping terrorist attacks.

Counterterrorism agents act as a bridge between the intelligence agencies, the police, and the government. They carefully track the latest scientific and political developments, and offer advice on how best to deal with the terrorist threat to US interests.

Forensic scientists play a huge part in investigating deadly acts of terrorism.

*Following a terrorist attack, every shred of **evidence** is searched for so it can be scientifically tested.*

Protecting the Public

With the rise of global terrorism in recent decades, protecting the public is now a priority for governments, and every year, billions of dollars are invested in preventing terrorist attacks. Much of the funds are directed toward scientific research into technology and methods that can help fight the war on terror.

USING SCIENCE TO SOLVE CRIMES

Science is vital to the teams trying to **foil** terrorist plans, and find out who is responsible for them if they do occur. There are many forensic science techniques that can be used to examine evidence at the sight of attacks, and new science is being developed all the time to help agents learn more about terrorism and how to prevent it.

Understanding Terrorism

Before terrorists can be stopped, investigators must know who they are and what **motivates** them. Learning this is one of the key jobs of forensic scientists and special agents who work in counterterrorism. Counterterrorism is anything done to "counter" the terrorist threat to a particular country. That can mean preventing acts of terrorism, capturing terrorists, and investigating terrorist attacks.

No Easy Task

Working in counterterrorism is a high-pressure job. A single mistake could result in a terrorist attack that kills hundreds or even thousands of people. Terrorists are constantly creating new ways to make deadly weapons, so counterterrorism workers need to stay ahead of their enemy. Terrorists also do everything they can to avoid detection, so it is a constant battle to uncover terrorist plans.

Terrorists do their best to look like ordinary people, in order to avoid detection.

*Spy **satellites** are one of the US government's biggest weapons in the war on terror.*

Terrorism Teams

Counterterrorism is an incredibly complicated world. In the United States alone, many thousands of people are employed in the counterterrorism departments of the FBI and CIA. Some are scientists performing tests to detect deadly germs that could be used by terrorists. Others are working on top-secret projects or are computer **analysts** charged with keeping track of emails between suspected terrorists.

CRIME SCIENCE

Counterterrorism scientists work specifically on projects that deal with the threat of terrorism. Some scientists are charged with discovering new, cutting-edge forensic techniques to help in the detection of planned attacks. Others carry out research into chemicals that could be used as weapons. Their work is highly secretive, but vital in ensuring the safety of us all.

7

Terror and Religion

Many terrorist attacks are carried out in the name of religion. There are people around the world who believe they are in a "holy war" against those with different religious views. Often, they are prepared to die for their extreme religious beliefs and because of this, they are very dangerous.

Deadly Cells

Terrorists are often organized into **cells**. These are groups that plan and carry out attacks. The methods used in these attacks vary, from hijacking planes to taking **hostages**, but most include the use of homemade bombs, which are often made from household items. Finding terror cells and figuring out how they plan to make bombs are two of the biggest challenges facing counterterrorism officials.

The tension between religions in the Middle East has inspired many acts of terrorism.

On US Soil

Many of the deadliest terror attacks the world has ever seen have been the work of religious **extremists**. The 9/11 attacks, the most high-profile terrorist acts on US soil, were the work of a small group of people who believe in an extreme form of Islam. The "**fundamentalists**" who were responsible for the 9/11 attacks were part of a terrorist organization called Al-Qaeda. The group waged a war against the West, especially Christian and Jewish people, and was led by the infamous Osama bin Laden. He inspired terrorist fighters to take up the war against the West, claiming they were fighting a "holy war."

The terrorist attacks on the twin towers in 2001 led to one of the biggest terrorist-hunt missions in history.

TRUE CRIME STORY

The capturing of Osama bin Laden after the 9/11 attacks was made an absolute priority by the US government. It resulted in one of the biggest **surveillance** operations in US history. Over a period of six months, the CIA used satellites and unmanned **drone** planes to film bin Laden's home, which was a **compound** in Pakistan. That information was used to mount a raid on the compound, which led to the killing of the Al-Qaeda leader.

Not Just Religion

Not all terrorists are religious extremists. Some hold extreme political views, or are motivated to plan acts of terror because of their belief in a particular cause. In the United States, these types of terrorists are not particularly common, but they exist. However, in other parts of the world, they are far more widespread.

Acts of Terror

There are many smaller terrorist groups that gain inspiration from extreme views or their belief in a particular cause. For example, the FBI **monitors white nationalist** groups in the United States, which are motivated by a belief that people of color are inferior. Another area of concern are groups claiming to protect animals used in scientific research. They include the Animal Rights Militia (ARM) and Animal Liberation Front (ALF). Both have carried out acts of terror.

Terror Against Scientists

A number of scientists who work in animal-testing laboratories have been harmed by letter bombs that were sent to their homes. When investigating letter-bomb attacks by animal rights groups, the police and forensic scientists will dust for fingerprints and test for **deoxyribonucleic acid (DNA)**.

Lone Wolves

Although terrorist groups are secretive, it is possible to uncover their plans by monitoring their emails or placing undercover agents within their cells. However, when terrorists act alone, this is not possible. Terrorists who act alone are called lone wolves. Most lone-wolf terrorists have extreme views, but they do not always air them in public until after their attacks. This can make detecting them impossible, and result in terrible consequences.

Often, little is known about a lone-wolf terrorist, so officers must be prepared for anything when attempting to arrest the terrorist.

TRUE CRIME STORY

In 2022, a heavily armed young, white male gunned down 13 people in Buffalo, New York. He chose a neighborhood in which many African Americans lived to carry out the shootings, and is reported to have avoided shooting white people. Throughout the incident, he recorded his actions and livestreamed them. Counterterrorist agents later learned that the lone wolf had deeply racist views, which had been inspired by material that he had found online.

It can be difficult to uncover the unusual and unpredictable plans of lone wolf terrorists.

STOP THE RADICAL

Many terrorists who have committed acts of terror, either as part of a terrorist cell or as a lone wolf, were inspired by information they read on the Internet. Terrorist groups use the Internet to spread their messages, and persuade people to join their causes. This is known as radicalization. Counterterrorism agents are aware of the threat posed by radicalization, and have developed a number of methods to **counteract** it.

Around the World

Many countries around the world, including Denmark, Germany, and the United Kingdom (UK), have developed deradicalization programs to help deal with the problem of terrorism in their countries. A similar program has been developed in Minnesota. It began in 2016, building on a system of using **mentors** to work with young **Somali** men who had been persuaded to try and leave the United States to fight for the terrorist organization known as the **Islamic State of Iraq and Syria (ISIS)**. The program has since developed into a model that is used to work with white nationalists, a group that is becoming an increasingly worrying terrorist threat within the United States.

Crime Science

Deradicalization has arisen from an understanding that trying to simply wipe out terrorists as a means of stopping terrorism does not work. If one terrorist is killed, it often inspires others to take their place and take up the cause—the dead terrorist becomes a **martyr** and symbol of the cause. Deradicalization instead tries to shift people's ways of thinking and explores the root causes of **extremism**.

Understanding Deradicalization

Deradiacalization involves working with people to try and **reform** them by challenging their extremist views. People are offered **counseling**, discussion, education, and mentoring to help them reassess what they have learned and explore new viewpoints. The method encourages individuals to **moderate** their beliefs and avoid violence as a means of expressing their religious viewpoints.

Today, many people who work in counterterrorism agree that trying to work with radicalized people rather than simply locking them up is a better solution to the problem of radicalization.

13

TRACKING TERRORISM

The Internet has made it possible for people all over the world to be connected to each other, but it has also made it possible for terrorists scattered in **remote** places around the world to plan attacks that will lead to devastation and deaths.

Eyes on the Net

Due to the increased threat of terrorism attacks in recent years, government counterterrorism agencies devote a lot of time to monitoring the Internet. This can take many forms, from checking websites run by fundamentalists to monitoring online sales of materials used in the making of homemade bombs.

Monitoring communications on the Internet helps agents keep watch for any suspected terrorist activity.

Not all terrorist attacks are possible to track via the Internet, but intercepting any activity can help prevent attacks that devastate communities.

Seeking Suspects

Counterterrorism agents use a special technique called traffic analysis to monitor the online discussions of suspected terrorists. Traffic analysis means watching the frequency of emails between two or more suspected terrorists in order to figure out what they are planning. If a lot of emails are sent and received in a short space of time, it could mean that an attack is being planned.

CRIME SCIENCE

Government counterterrorism agents also use another technique known as packet sniffing to help them monitor communications across the Internet. Packet sniffing, also sometimes called packet **analyzing,** involves using computer **software** to track and record everything that passes across a selected computer network, for example, those used by people to access the Internet either at home or on the move.

15

Watching the Terrorists

Once a suspected or known terrorist has been identified, counterterrorism agents will use all the scientific tools they have to keep track of them. This can mean using surveillance techniques that were previously used only by the armed services.

Listen and Learn

The armed services have access to powerful tools that they use to watch and track terrorists. The US government has listening stations throughout the world, which use powerful listening devices to pick up cell phone calls and radio communications. The US government also uses satellites, positioned hundreds of miles above Earth, to film suspected terrorist activity on the ground.

Eyes in the Sky

Most modern cell phones regularly communicate with the **Global Positioning System (GPS)**. This system is used by millions of people around the world every day, and can also be used to monitor the movement of terrorists. GPS allows electronic devices to calculate their exact position by sending and receiving signals to a network of satellites. If the cell phone number of a suspected terrorist is known, their movements can be tracked using the GPS network.

*Satellite surveillance has helped agents pinpoint the exact **location** of known terrorists.*

TRUE CRIME STORY

In 2022, the US military carried out a strike against the leader who took control of Al-Qaeda after the death of Osama bin Laden. His name was Ayman al-Zawahiri, and the attack took place in Kabul, Afghanistan. The military were able to use incredibly precise coordinates to fire two missiles at the terrorist group leader while he stood on his balcony, while leaving his wife and daughter (who were inside the building) unharmed. Counterterrorism agents had been monitoring the Al-Qaeda leader for months before the attack, using state-of-the-art surveillance technology to track his movements and daily habits. That intelligence allowed military **personnel** to launch the incredibly efficient attack.

An unmanned drone such as this was used to fire the missiles that killed Ayman al-Zawahiri in 2022.

Many agents spend most of their week listening to phone calls or trawling through emails from suspected terrorists.

High-Tech Hunting

Counterterrorism agents watch the Internet to monitor the movements of terrorists. They also use a number of high-tech methods to keep track of telephone calls made and received by people who are suspected of being involved in terrorist activity.

Tracking Calls

The United States National Security Agency (NSA) records basic details of all phone calls made and received by customers of the country's four biggest telephone companies. Details of numbers dialed, calls received, and call lengths are stored on a massive bank of computers in what is known as a call database. Counterterrorism agents use the database to find out who is making and receiving calls from suspected terrorists.

Which Phone?

Call databases can be useful to counterterrorism agents, but their vast size makes them difficult to handle. This is why CIA and FBI agents use pen registers to track the phone calls of suspected terrorists. A pen register records and decodes the numbers called by a particular fixed line or cell phone used by a suspect.

CRIME SCIENCE

During counterterrorism operations, wire-tapping devices may also be used. These can record phone conversations between suspected criminals or terrorists. Wire-tapping is usually used to collect evidence. Occasionally, video cameras or other recording devices may be placed in the homes of suspected terrorists.

Hidden Weapons

Many counterterrorism officials think that the greatest terrorist threat in the future may not come from bombs, but rather chemical and biological weapons. These include poisonous gases and deadly germs that could kill hundreds of thousands of people.

Chemical Wars

It is not difficult to create poisonous gases in a laboratory, and the CIA believes that some terror groups may already have this capability. They are not yet sure that terrorists are able to create germs that will make people very sick, but they have to be prepared for the possibility.

Germ Warfare

One of the problems facing scientists is that germs and poison gases are often colorless and odorless. If a terrorist released germs or poison in a crowded place, it would be difficult to detect them. To help identify if gases have been released, scientists have developed biodetectors. These are chemicals that change appearance if a certain gas or germ is present. They can be put inside devices carried by **field agents**, so that the agents can detect poison threats.

If terrorists set off a biological weapon in a subway train, hundreds of people could die.

CRIME SCIENCE

Most biodetectors include some type of living organism—for example, a germ—that changes its appearance in the presence of a particular poison. Biodetectors are far more sensitive to poisonous substances than humans, which means they can detect them long before they may do us any harm.

21

OUTWIT THE TERRORIST

In a world in which terrorist threats are constantly changing, counterterrorist agents need to be armed with knowledge about all possible means of attack that terrorists could use. In counterterrorism labs, scientists dedicate themselves to understanding potential terrorism methods. Governments invest millions of dollars every year in counterterrorism research, employing some of the most talented scientists in the country to investigate new forensic techniques that could help agents learn more about terrorist attacks.

Forensic Finds

One of the key areas of research carried out by counterterrorism labs is chemical analysis. This involves closely examining chemical substances, both natural and man-made, how they work, and if they could potentially be used in weapons. For example, counterterrorism scientists carry out experiments to find out whether household items, such as soft-drink cans, batteries, and bleach, can be used to make bombs. They also investigate what ingredients could be used to make a dirty bomb, which is a mixture of explosives such as dynamite and radioactive powder or pellets. And if a terrorist bomb attack does take place, forensic scientists often carry out a chemical analysis on remains to find out how the bomb was made.

Hidden Threats

Counterterrorism scientists also carry out experiments to find out what types of new virus strains terrorists may try and develop in their own labs, and what impact those strains would have if they were used in a biological warfare attack. They also research chemicals and how they could be used to create chemical weapons that would deliver a deadly assault.

Crime Science

Today, many forensic scientists working in counterterrorist labs are taught using innovative **virtual reality (VR)** tools that immerse them in a terrorist lab. In the lab, the scientists can interact virtually and learn how terrorists could use science to create **lethal** weapons.

Scientists gather and examine microscopic evidence to discover how terrorists carried out an attack.

CRIME SCIENCE

Artificial Intelligence (AI) is a term used to describe a computer or another machine that can perform tasks only a human being could usually complete. Many counterterrorism agencies are now concerned that terrorists could use AI to carry out acts of terror. They believe that AI could be used to carry out physical attacks—for example, using self-driving cars or drones—or to carry out cybercrimes, such as attacking websites or spreading messages of hate and encouraging violence via the Internet.

Could drones be the method of choice for future terror attacks?

Devastating Destruction

The prospect of terrorists gaining access to and using **weapons of mass destruction (WOMD)** is a very real threat, and one that concerns governments around the world. Over the years, terrorist groups have tested new ways to get access to and use WOMD to wreak devastation on their targets.

A Dark Place

The dark web is an area of the Internet in which **illegal** activity takes place. Counterterrorist agents are increasingly aware that terrorists could use the dark web to buy material to make WOMD, or gain access to the weapons themselves. Counterterrorist organizations around the world now work together to monitor and stop possible WOMD terrorist activities, including stopping the smuggling of materials that could be used to make weapons, the buying and selling of WOMD, and how to coordinate a response if WOMD were ever used to carry out a terrorist attack.

Tiny Weapons

The CIA also believes that organized terror groups may attempt to use nanotechnology to create bombs. Nanotechnology is technology so small it can be seen only under a microscope. Currently, the creation of bombs with nanotechnology is unlikely. However, because it may be possible in the future, the US government is funding research into the development of nanotech weapons. If terrorists did try to use nanotechnology, the government hopes to be able to foil their plans.

Counterterrorist scientists have developed robots that help bomb-disposal experts safely diffuse bombs.

CHAPTER 3

AFTER AN ATTACK

Although counterterrorism agents work incredibly hard to prevent terrorist attacks, they are not always successful. If a terrorist attack does take place, it is the role of crime scene investigators, federal agents, and forensic scientists to attempt to figure out what happened, why it happened, and who was behind it.

A Terrible Task

Whether they are police officers, federal agents, or forensic scientists, nobody wants to have to investigate a terrorist attack. If they are sent to the scene of a terrorist attack, there is a strong chance that many people will have been killed or injured, and that is distressing to see.

Firefighters must secure the scene of a terrorist attack, putting out any fires, before investigators can begin their work.

Looking for Clues

Investigating a terrorist attack can take a long time. If many people have died, counterterrorism scientists will need to look for evidence that will help them determine how each person died. Investigators also look for clues that could show how the attack was carried out. For example, was it a bombing, and if so, what was used to make the bomb? Were the terrorists killed in the attack or are they still at large?

Extreme Science

When investigating acts of terrorism, counterterrorism scientists need to find evidence that will lead them to those behind the attacks. In extreme circumstances, such as bombings, they may also need to use all of their scientific skills to identify victims. Many of the methods they use are similar to those of regular forensic scientists.

CRIME SCIENCE

When arriving at the scene of a terrorist attack, counterterrorism scientists must carefully examine the crime scene. If it has been a particularly large attack, this may take days, weeks, or even months. They will take photographs and carefully collect evidence, before taking it to a laboratory for testing.

What and Why

When an explosion takes place, counterterrorism scientists must act quickly to investigate it. Sometimes, explosions occur naturally, for example, following a gas leak, but occasionally, a bomb planted by a terrorist is the cause. Whatever the cause, counterterrorism scientists must find out what happened and, most importantly, why it happened.

Bombed buildings can be very badly damaged and it can take investigators a long time to find out what happened there.

Searching for Evidence

Some scientists specialize in explosives. After a terrorist bomb blast, they will look for evidence to find out what caused the explosion. The area around the bomb site will be carefully examined for fragments, or pieces, of the bomb, gunpowder dust, traces of explosive, and wires and elements that could have been used to make a timing device. Marks on rubble and nearby structures can also be used to help pinpoint the exact location where the bomb was placed and detonated.

Back in the Lab

Forensic scientists must collect as much evidence as they can to take back to the laboratory. Once there, any fragments found will be tested to figure out exactly what was used to make the bomb. These fragments will also be examined to see if they contain the bomber's fingerprints or DNA. Forensic methods are now so advanced that it is sometimes even possible to figure out exactly where and when the bomb was made.

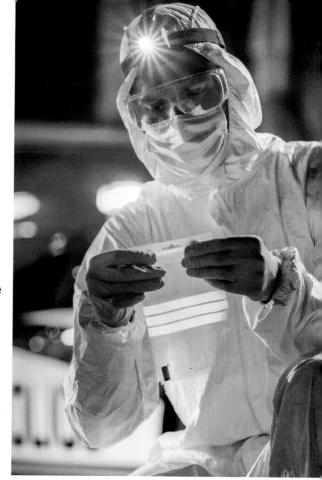

Any evidence found at a bomb site must be bagged and noted as part of a criminal investigation.

CRIME SCIENCE

If counterterrorists do manage to locate a bomb such as a pipe bomb before it explodes, dismantling the bomb is very dangerous—one wrong move and it could explode. However, for a state-of-the-art robot named SAPBER (Semi-Autonomous Pipe Bomb End-cap Remover), it is a much less dramatic task. The robot is designed to carefully take apart the bomb without disturbing the deadly explosive materials inside, which are carefully emptied. The materials and the pipe are kept as evidence, which can then later be examined in the lab. SAPBER has made dealing with terrorist bombs a far less risky procedure and ensured that vital evidence is collected for scientific investigation.

DNA Detectives

Another tool available to counterterrorism scientists is deoxyribonucleic acid (DNA) testing. This is the most accurate and advanced **identification** system—it is said to be accurate in 99 percent of cases. This means that, should DNA evidence exist, it will be almost impossible for a terrorist to escape identification.

Impossible to Fake

DNA is a unique code that is found in every human body cell. Every single person's DNA is different, and it is impossible to fake. Traces of DNA can be found in body parts, hair, teeth, and the tiny skin cells left by terrorists at crime scenes. If a suspected terrorist is arrested, the police will carry out a DNA test to determine whether it matches any traces of DNA found at the crime scene. In cases where a terrorist has died in a bomb blast, DNA can also be used to identify them.

DNA testing is a long and complicated process, but it can help investigators identify terrorists.

Mitochondria for the Missing

It is also possible to identify human remains, such as bones and teeth, using a process called **mitochondrial DNA** testing. This can be very useful to counterterrorism scientists when the fire following a bomb blast has destroyed most of the evidence. Mitochondrial DNA testing is a slow process, and is not nearly as accurate as regular DNA testing, but it is still accurate enough to identify missing people following a terrorist attack.

Mitochondrial DNA testing is often used to identify people using just their bones or teeth, for example, after a natural disaster such as a wildfire.

TRUE CRIME STORY

DNA testing on human remains found in the aftermath of the 9/11 attacks in New York City has helped identify 1,633 of the estimated 2,753 people who died during the attacks. In the months following 9/11, DNA was taken from surviving family members and used to identify the remains of **victims** of the attacks. The groundbreaking work carried out after 9/11 has since developed to such a great extent that people can now be identified within a matter of hours. It is called Rapid DNA technology and has been used to identify victims of other disasters that have occurred since 9/11, including wildfire disasters in California.

RECOGNIZE BIOMETRICS

DNA testing is not the only way of identifying suspected terrorists. In recent years, resources have been invested in "biometrics," which is the use of characteristics to identify people using film and photographs. Biometrics can include a person's facial features, the shape of their face, and even the way they walk, sit, and smell!

Crime Science

Today, many countries are increasingly sharing biometric data in an attempt to stop terrorism. By sharing the data, it is possible to carry out more biometric tests at borders and monitor suspects entering and leaving countries. This wider sharing of information and greater cooperation makes it far more difficult for terrorists to carry out their plans.

Biometric technology measures the dimensions of different parts of a person's face to identify them.

Passport Photos

The most common application of biometrics is in passports. For example, US passports issued today include a **microchip** that stores statistics about the passport holder's facial features, such as the shape of their face, length of nose, eye color, and so on. Some airports now make people walk through biometric scanners on arrival, to make sure that the person entering the country is who they say they are. In addition, a photograph is now taken of everyone who enters the United States. This is kept on record for 75 years and can be used to make a biometric profile if needed.

Checking Suspects

When DNA evidence is not available, biometrics can be extremely valuable to counterterrorism agents. It has allowed them to accurately identify terrorist suspects from a distance, using surveillance cameras and satellite images. If there is a picture of a suspect on file, it can be cross-checked with a new photograph or film footage. This technique is used by the military when identifying suspects in countries where there is a high level of suspicious activity.

Attacks in the Air

Some of the worst terrorist attacks of recent years have involved aircraft. Terrorists often target planes because they are unprotected, and when they crash, it is likely that hundreds of people will die. When a terrorist causes a plane to explode or crash, it is the work of aircraft-accident investigators to piece together what happened—and why.

Find the Box

Investigations into aircraft accidents and crashes within the United States are the responsibility of the National Transportation Safety Board (NTSB). They have a team of experts whose job it is to examine all available evidence to determine the cause of any incidents, whether deadly or not. The first task for the investigators is to recover the flight recorder and cabin voice recorder. These two steel boxes are fitted to each aircraft and should contain all the information needed to figure out whether an airplane was hijacked or bombed, or if it crashed due to technical failure within the plane.

Piecing It Together

Even when investigators know for sure that an airplane has been bombed, they still need to piece together the exact details of how the explosion happened and destroyed the plane. In this instance, they often try to recover as much wreckage as possible to examine it for clues.

TRUE CRIME STORY

After an airplane carrying many US passengers exploded directly over the town of Lockerbie in Scotland in 1988, air-crash investigators collected the wreckage and transported it to a hangar in England. There, they were able to put the plane back together, piece by piece.

When they did this, investigators discovered a 66-feet- (20 m) wide hole in the underside of the front cargo hold. From this, they deduced that a bomb had been placed in a suitcase. A Libyan man named Abu Agila Mohammad Masud was accused of making the bomb, and the hunt for him commenced. Finally, in 2022, Masud was taken into US custody.

Flight recorders help determine what happened in the event of a crash or terrorist attack.

If an airplane crashes over water, this is often not possible. Then, focus will switch back to finding the flight recorder, which may be the only means of discovering what happened.

Although terrorists often target planes, successful attacks are still a rarity.

CHAPTER 4

CONTROLLING TERRORISM

If you were asked to describe a typical terrorist, where would you begin? One of the most difficult aspects of terrorist control is that terrorists appear to be ordinary people who are going about everyday lives. Terrorists live within the countries they wish to attack, within their communities. They are highly organized and can change their plans at speed to outwit counterterrorism units. This is why it is so hard to control terrorism.

Cat and Mouse

Most terrorists and terror groups cannot afford to spend the vast amounts of money that governments can invest in scientific research to counteract terrorism. However, that does not mean that terrorists cannot come up with complex bomb plots or develop new weapons using cutting-edge scientific techniques. Terrorists are also always looking for any weaknesses within a country's defenses, whether they are at airports, stadiums, or shopping malls. To prevent attacks, agents must predict all possible terrorist actions. It is an ongoing game of cat and mouse.

Airport security has been tightened in response to the increased threat of terrorism worldwide.

Armed police response teams are trained to know what to do in the event of a terrorist attack.

Step by Step

Together, people and organizations are working to take steps to defeat terrorism. Scientists are constantly perfecting new methods of searching the Internet for information about planned terrorist activity. Government agencies, private firms, and international organizations are spending billions of dollars every year on scientific research programs into key areas of counterterrorism. Because of this, breakthrough inventions that can improve security worldwide are introduced all the time.

CRIME SCIENCE

Subways, music concert and sports venues, and airports are just some of the places that terrorists target when they carry out their attacks. NATO has developed a system for countering these threats called DEXTER, which is short for Detection of Explosives and firearms to counter TERrorism.

The technology scans everybody who passes into an area for explosives or firearms, while still allowing the free flow of people. It can pick up a firearm hidden beneath clothing or in a bag, or a secreted explosive. If any threat is detected, counterterrorist agents will immediately pick it up and act.

Safety in the Air

Since traveling on airplanes first became popular in the early 1970s, terrorists have chosen to target airliners. Many of the worst terrorist attacks of the last 40 years have involved terrorists either blowing up, crashing, or hijacking planes. As a result, billions of dollars have been spent on airport security in order to try and keep airplane passengers safe.

Tighter Security

Up until 1972, it was possible to board a plane without having any bags checked. Then, following a high-profile terrorist hijacking, the US government ordered all US airports to install metal detectors. Today, airport security is tighter than ever before, including X-ray machines that allow staff to look for suspicious items inside bags without needing to open them.

Airport "sniffer" dogs are trained to sniff out explosives, drugs, and firearms.

Body scanners are used to search people traveling through airports.

In-Flight Danger

Full-body scanner machines use invisible radio waves to create a three-dimensional (3-D) computer image. By doing this, security staff can see whether travelers are hiding drugs, weapons, and explosives. This is just one example of how airport security is responding to the threat of terrorism. In 2006, the CIA uncovered a plot to use plastic bottles in a terrorist attack. Since then, it has been illegal to carry plastic bottles of more than 3.4 fluid ounces (100 ml) onto an airplane.

CRIME SCIENCE

Currently, airport travelers must remove any liquids such as water bottles from their carry-on baggage before going on a flight. However, soon many airports may drop the restrictions around carrying such liquids thanks to new high-tech security scanning.

In many airports in the near future, 3-D scanners will be able to scan luggage in such detail that any concerning substances will be picked up and an alert given, and non-concerning substances will simply pass through.

SCAN THE FUTURE

Science and technology develops so quickly that it is difficult to keep up. To ensure that they stay one step ahead of the terrorists, governments throughout the world need to make sure they keep abreast of all developments, however small. To do so, they employ people called horizon scanners. Counterterrorism horizon scanners divide their time between reading reports from scientists, gathering information from counterterrorism agents, and writing advice for the government.

Watching and Predicting

The concept of "horizon scanning" is simple. It means closely watching scientific developments in order to predict future discoveries. For example, if one group of scientists discovers a new type of chemical, horizon-scanning experts would note this and think about how it might be used in the future. It could be that the chemical has potential to be used to make a bomb. It is the job of horizon scanners to figure this out before any terrorists do.

Gathering Intel

There are two cutting-edge techniques experts say will be important in the future of counterterrorism: data mining and algorithms. Data mining is a way of sifting through huge amounts of information to find specific things. For example, data mining can be used to search for money transfers and communications that could be linked to terrorism. It can also be used to identify and track terrorists, by checking their travel and immigration records. That data can lead counterterrorism agents directly to the terrorists, and help them monitor their activities.

Crime Science

Data mining involves collecting huge amounts of information about people and then storing it on computers. This information can be analyzed using software programs called databases. Counterterrorism agents can then use the databases to search for people who fit the profile of suspected terrorists, such as known religious fundamentalists who have been buying plane tickets to and from countries suspected of supporting terrorism.

Horizon-scanning experts must keep up to date with all the latest scientific developments.

Predicting the Future

Algorithms and mathematical models use information about people to predict how they may behave and what future events may occur. For example, they try and predict whether a terrorist will use a weapon, if their act of terror is likely to succeed or fail, where the attack will take place, and what form it will occur in—for example, a bombing or an airplane hijack.

THE FUTURE OF TERRORISM

Today, terrorism is a very real threat in almost every country around the world. As a result, more resources than ever before are being poured into counterterrorism to keep people safe. Governments are working internationally to join forces against terrorism, and are sharing the scientific advances made within their countries to assist each other.

Science in the Fight

In the last four decades, science has helped tackle terrorism in many ways, from the development of accurate DNA and biometrics testing to the use of drones for surveillance and full-body scanners at airports. Through the use of these inventions and others, many terrorists have been arrested and put on trial for their crimes, or stopped before they could carry out their plans.

Terrorist attacks wreak devastation on the victims' families. People working in counterterrorism are committed to stopping these appalling acts.

Into the Future

There are still many challenges ahead for the counterterrorism agents charged with keeping people safe. Finding and monitoring terrorists in the Internet age is becoming increasingly problematic, and there is still much we still do not know about the true extent of the threat from biological and chemical weapons. Terrorists will never stop plotting new ways to harm people, so counterterrorism scientists must keep working hard to develop new ways to find, stop, and help convict terrorists.

MAKE CRIME SCIENCE YOUR FUTURE

Working in counterterrorism is a fast-paced field. Having a well-developed understanding of latest scientific and technological breakthroughs and how a terrorist could use them is essential. If you think you have what it takes to work in this cutting-edge field, overleaf you'll find a career guide that could help you one day foil a terrorist attack.

CRIME-STOPPING CAREERS

COULD YOU HELP FIGHT TERRORISM?

Crime dramas win record viewings, and these gripping shows have inspired many to enter the world of crime science and investigation. It is an amazingly exciting field to work in, with new, game-changing developments emerging all the time.

The work of forensic scientists working in counterterrorism is varied, from computer forensics and crime scene analysis through **toxicology**. There are several organizations that have counterterrorism jobs available, such as the CIA and FBI. The below chart outlines some of the areas of counterterroism work.

Working in Counterterrorism

- Identification of bodies after a terrorist attack
- Analysis of crime scene evidence
- Detection of biological warfare substances
- Analysis of poisonous substances
- Forensic examination of computers
- Analysis of explosives and drugs

To pursue a career in counterterrorism, follow this simple flowchart.

Focus on STEM subjects at school

Science subjects are particularly important for future careers in counterterrorism.

↓

Choose a career area to specialize in

There are several different areas that you can focus on in the field of counterterrorism, so you may want to decide now what type of job you'd like in the future.

↓

Earn a bachelor's degree

This is a requirement for some jobs in the industry, but there are some roles that will consider a high-school diploma or associate's degree. The degree should be relevant to the role you want. Subjects such as criminology, psychology, law enforcement, or forensic science are sometimes requested, depending on the role you are interested in.

↓

Consider additional study or training

Depending on your chosen job, additional training or study may be required. This may be a master's degree or a doctorate, or a specialized course offered by the organization you wish to work for. Sometimes, an ability to speak foreign languages is requested too.

↓

Apply for jobs

Apply for your first job. Some roles require additional job experience, so you may need to work in another role until you have the experience to apply. There are also jobs that will require a certain level of security clearance or require overseas travel, so check the requirements carefully.

GLOSSARY

analysts people who carefully study something

analyzing studying something carefully in order to better understand it

cells small groups of terrorists

compound a highly secure home that people live in for protection

counseling guidance to help work through emotional issues

counteract to make ineffective

counterterrorism agents people whose job it is to monitor terrorists and foil any plans they make

deoxyribonucleic acid (DNA) the unique code inside every human body cell that controls every element of how we look

drone an unmanned aircraft that is often used to gather information

evidence information, objects, or substances that are related to a crime

extremism promoting extreme views

extremists people who have and promote extreme views

field agents agents who operate outside of an office

foil to stop a plan

forensic applying scientific knowledge to solve criminal and legal problems

fundamentalists people with extreme views, sometimes based on particular interpretations of religious teachings

Global Positioning System (GPS) a navigational system using satellite signals to fix the location of a radio receiver on or above Earth's surface

hostages people taken by force to secure the taker's demands

identification figuring out who someone is

illegal against the law

intelligence information concerning an enemy or potential enemy

Islamic State of Iraq and Syria (ISIS) a militant Islamic group

lethal resulting in death

location the place where something is found or where something occurs

martyr a person who sacrifices their life for the sake of a principle

mentors trusted counselors or guides

microchip a circuit integrated within something

mitochondrial DNA DNA found in mitochondria, the tiniest parts of cells

moderate to lessen extreme views

monitors checks or keeps watch over

motivates creates a strong desire to do something

personnel people who work for an organization

reform to change and improve

remote far away and difficult to reach

satellites man-made devices sent into space for specific purposes

software computer programs that tell a computer what to do

Somali a person from Somalia, Africa

surveillance keeping a close watch over someone or something

toxicology a science that deals with poisons and their effects

victims people who have been injured, harmed, or killed by other people

virtual reality (VR) an artificial environment created by a computer

weapons of mass destruction (WOMD) weapons that can destroy entire regions

white nationalist a person who believes that white people are superior to people of color

FIND OUT MORE

Books

Boutland, Craig. *The War on Terror: Timelines, Facts, and Battles* (America Goes to War). Rosen Publishing, 2023.

Campbell, Grace. *Crime Scene Evidence* (True Crime Clues). Lerner Publishing, 2021.

Cooper, Chris. *Forensic Science: Discover the Fascinating Methods Scientists Use to Solve Crimes* (DK Eyewitness). DK Children, 2020.

Edwards, Sue Bradford. *The Dark Web* (Privacy in the Digital Age). Core Library, 2019.

Websites

Find out more about counterterrorism around the world at:
academickids.com/encyclopedia/index.php/Counterterrorism

Discover a great introduction to the world of forensic science, featuring explanations of many of the techniques mentioned in this book at:
www.all-about-forensic-science.com

For details of how you can try some forensic science techniques at home, visit:
www.explainthatstuff.com/forensicscience.html

Visit the FBI website to find out more about cybercrime at:
www.fbi.gov/investigate/cyber

Publisher's note to educators and parents:
All the websites featured above have been carefully reviewed to ensure that they are suitable for students. However, many websites change often, and we cannot guarantee that a site's future contents will continue to meet our high standards of educational value. Please be advised that students should be closely monitored whenever they access the Internet.

INDEX

About the Author

Sarah Eason is an experienced children's book author who has written many science books for children. She loves watching crime-detective shows, and after researching and writing this book is more fascinated than ever by the world of counterterrorism and forensic science.